STEPS TO RETIRE AND STAY STRONG

Building a Good retirement

Rosendo A. Price

Introduction

Setting off on the path to retirement involves a significant change in lifestyle and purpose in addition to monetary adjustments. The closer people get to this big turning point, the more important it is to prepare carefully. In order to make sure that the golden years are full of meaning, happiness, and continuous development, we dig into the nuances of retiring in this book.

Although retirement is sometimes seen as a time for leisure and relaxation, there are several traps to watch out for that may result in stagnation—or, to put it more dramatically, the sensation of slowly fading away. The goal of this book is to provide a thorough road map that covers the psychological, social, physical, and financial facets of a successful retirement.

We will discuss the value of maintaining a healthy lifestyle, creating social bonds, seeking lifelong learning, and partaking in fulfilling activities throughout these processes.People may proactively mould their post-career years into a time of self-discovery and significant contributions by approaching retirement with a holistic mentality.

Join us as we explore the many facets of retirement, providing advice, ideas, and tactics to make sure that your golden years are more than simply a time off from work—rather, they should be a dynamic chapter full of connections, purpose, and a passion for life. Let's get started on the processes that will lead you to a retirement where your goals go beyond just getting by—into the most rewarding life conceivable.

Retired Life

Being retired is a big change that gives people a chance to welcome a new stage of life that is defined by fulfillment, relaxation, and self-discovery.It's a period when retirees may enjoy the rewards of their retirement as the hectic pace of work life gives way to a gentler one. In order to provide a pleasant living free from the restraints of work-related commitments, financial preparation becomes essential.

Reevaluating one's priorities and objectives is a common reaction to retirement. Some decide to take a trip, seeing places they had previously had to put off because of business obligations. Some engage in hobbies, unearthing latent passions or reviving long-forgotten interests. A feeling of independence and autonomy is fostered in retirees by having no set timetable to follow and the ability to manage their time as they see fit.

In retirement, having social ties is essential. Retirees prioritise maintaining and building connections, often participating in volunteer work, attending community events, and spending time with friends and family. These relationships strengthen the foundation of a strong support network, which improves mental and emotional health at this point in life.

As retirees realize how crucial it is to have balanced lives, health takes the central stage. A healthy diet, regular exercise, and preventative healthcare become essential elements of retirement, guaranteeing lifespan and improved quality of life. A holistic approach to health is promoted by the goal of wellbeing, which goes beyond physical well-being to include mental and emotional components.

Although it's often linked to retirement, financial security is just one aspect of this complex stage. A feeling of purpose, personal development, and emotional health are all equally important. Retired people could look into new educational options, engage in artistic activities, or even launch a second profession out of love rather than need.

Managing the emotional elements of retirement may be difficult, and some people struggle with a loss of identity connected to their work duties. It's an opportunity to examine oneself and realize that worth goes beyond professional accomplishments. Retirees may find comfort in taking on mentoring responsibilities, passing along their wealth of knowledge to the next generation, or making philanthropic contributions.

Essentially, retirement is a stage of life characterized by the coming together of recently acquired independence, personal growth, and the search for significant encounters. It's a chance to write a story that inspires people to embrace and appreciate the wide range of possibilities in life, breaking free from the limitations of the everyday grind.

Important of retirement

For a number of reasons, retirement is a big deal in people's lives. First of all, it marks the end of a long and devoted profession and gives people a chance to celebrate the results of their hard work. It makes it possible to go from the rigours of a full-time career to a period of leisure and personal interests.

An important part of retirement is financial planning, which emphasizes the need of making prudent investments and savings throughout one's working years to guarantee a safe and happy post-employment phase. Savings for retirement, such as 401(k) accounts and pension plans, are essential for maintaining a chosen lifestyle and paying for medical bills.

Retirement is an opportunity for personal development and inquiry as well. People may travel, take up hobbies, and do other things that they couldn't do while they were employed. This stage often offers retirees a feeling of contentment and self-discovery, enabling them to reevaluate their priorities and discover new joys.

Retirement planning is crucial because it gives people the time they need to prioritize their health. A longer, more satisfying retirement may be achieved by adopting a healthy lifestyle and effectively managing stress. Regular medical checkups also become essential throughout this time to quickly treat any health risks.

Making new friends is yet another important retirement feature. It becomes crucial to establish and keep up a solid support network for emotional health. The significance of relationships in achieving total life happiness is emphasised by the fact that retirees often feel pleasure in spending quality time with friends and family.

Retirement also has an effect on society as a whole. Younger generations may now join the workforce thanks to retirements, which encourages innovation and boosts the economy. Social security and labour market dynamics are also influenced by policies pertaining to retirement age and benefits.

To sum up, retirement is a complex stage of life that includes aspects related to finances, health, relationships, and social aspects. Its importance transcends the individual to impact larger social institutions, therefore careful retirement preparation and contemplation are essential for a well-rounded and satisfying life path.

Adjusting to Retirement

Retirement adjustment is a complex process that involves careful consideration of both pragmatic issues and the emotional terrain. When people say goodbye to their professional professions, they start a journey that requires them to adjust to a new habit, identity, and purpose.

First of all, it might be confusing to go from a set job schedule to an unstructured daily routine. It takes intentionality to create a post-retirement habit since retirees often struggle with the lack of obligations and deadlines. Establishing a flexible schedule that incorporates hobbies, important pursuits, and social events helps keep the newly acquired freedom from becoming monotonous.

Redefining one's identity is an essential part of retirement adjustment. Many people have a strong emotional connection between their professional duties and who they are. As retirement draws to an end, retirees are forced to consider their value and purpose in life. Recognising that worth goes beyond professional accomplishments and that retirees may find pleasure in a variety of pursuits, including family, hobbies, and community service, is a necessary step in this process.

Retirement also brings about changes in social relations. A more diverse network takes the role of the job, which is often the main area where people engage socially. It becomes essential to actively build new contacts, take part in community events, and remain in touch with loved ones in order to avoid loneliness and preserve a strong support network.

Making necessary financial changes is essential to adapting to retirement. Budgeting and careful financial preparation are necessary to guarantee a pleasant living even in the absence of a reliable source of income. To support their long-term financial objectives, retirees may need to review their spending patterns, look into possible passive income streams, and think about investing methods.

Priority one throughout the retirement transition process is emotional health. Emotions ranging from exhilaration to a feeling of bereavement might be brought on by the more free time. It might be difficult for retirees to find meaning and purpose outside of the workplace. Positive emotional adjustment is facilitated by self-reflection, following personal hobbies, and creating new objectives.

Retirement adaption emphasizes wellness and health. It is recommended that retirees make physical activity a priority, eat a healthy diet, and take an active role in their healthcare. In addition to improving wellbeing, a healthy lifestyle makes it possible for retirees to take full advantage of their newfound independence.

To sum up, transitioning to retirement is a complex process that needs an all-encompassing strategy. It entails reorganizing daily schedules, reinventing identity, fostering social ties, taking care of financial obligations, and placing an emphasis on one's physical and mental well-being. It takes a proactive attitude, perseverance, and an openness to seize the possibilities that retirement offers to successfully navigate this change.

Financial Planning

Financial planning is a thorough and deliberate process that people go through in order to successfully manage their financial resources, accomplish certain objectives, and ensure a safe and prosperous future. This complex field covers a number of topics, including investing, risk management, retirement planning, and estate planning in addition to budgeting.

Fundamentally, the first step in financial planning is to have a clear grasp of one's financial priorities. Setting clear financial objectives forms the cornerstone of any planning process, whether it house ownership, college finance, or a comfortable retirement. These objectives provide people direction when making decisions and help them allocate their resources sensibly.

A key component of financial planning is budgeting, which entails compiling a thorough summary of income and spending. People may find areas for possible savings and make sure their financial resources match their objectives by keeping track of and classifying their expenses. A well-designed budget is an effective instrument for maintaining financial self-control and attaining long-term prosperity.

Another important component of financial planning is investment planning, which maximizes asset accumulation over time. This includes determining one's level of risk tolerance, spreading one's assets among a range of asset classes, and keeping one's portfolio balanced. Investing in stocks, bonds, real estate, and other instruments helps to create and maintain financial assets. A well-thought-out investment plan is essential to this process.

A crucial factor in financial planning is risk management. This entails determining and reducing any financial risks, such as illness, incapacity, or sudden unemployment. Key elements of risk management include having enough emergency savings, insurance, and backup plans to maintain financial stability in the event of unanticipated events.

One long-term component of financial planning that calls for meticulous calculation and forethought is retirement planning. Important factors to take into mind include figuring out how much to save, selecting suitable retirement funds, and planning when to take retirement withdrawals. The goal of a well-designed retirement plan is to provide participants freedom and financial stability after retirement.

The process of estate planning entails transferring assets to designated beneficiaries in a systematic manner while reducing any tax consequences. One's legacy and the distribution of their money in accordance with their preferences are greatly influenced by their will, trust, and other legal documents.

In financial planning, tax planning is a continuous activity with the goal of maximizing tax efficiency. To reduce tax obligations, this entails studying pertinent tax laws, investigating credits and deductions, and carefully managing assets. One's whole financial picture may be greatly impacted by effective tax preparation.

It's critical to modify financial strategies in response to life events. Reevaluating financial objectives and tactics is necessary when facing unforeseen occurrences, marriage, childbirth, and job improvements. Individuals may make necessary modifications to their financial plans to remain on track towards their goals when they are flexible and examine them on a regular basis.

Financial planning is essentially a dynamic, ongoing process that calls for strategic thought, meticulous attention to detail, and a dedication to long-term financial well-being. It gives people the ability to take charge of their financial futures, deal with uncertainty, and strive towards a safe and successful present and future.

Pursuing Hobbies

Developing hobbies is more than just a recreational activity; it's a life-changing and rewarding experience. It entails making a conscious decision to devote time and effort to pursuits that make one happy, fulfilled, and give their life meaning. Hobbies are important because they may improve mental health, stimulate creativity, and lead to a meaningful and balanced life in addition to being enjoyable in and of themselves.

Having hobbies is a great way to escape the difficulties of everyday life and is a potent antidote to the demands of daily living. Hobbies, which might include painting, gardening, playing an instrument, or engaging in sports, provide a safe haven where people can fully engage in pursuits they are enthusiastic about, fostering relaxation and lessening the effects of stress.

Pursuing interests, developing latent abilities, and promoting original thought all foster creativity. Hobbies provide people a platform for self-expression and let them explore and develop their creative or imaginative side. In addition to providing personal fulfilment, this creative outlet improves problem-solving abilities and cognitive flexibility, which in turn improves general cognitive function.

Hobbies can have a social component that is notable. Making deep social relationships may be facilitated by participating in group activities or joining groups based on common interests. Developing connections with others who have similar interests promotes a feeling of community, fights feelings of loneliness, and builds a strong support system—all of which are essential for mental and emotional health.

Hobbies push people to develop and accomplish objectives, which promotes personal growth. Whether it's learning a new talent, finishing a difficult project, or hitting a fitness goal, pursuing hobbies fosters a feeling of success. In addition to raising self-esteem, this kind of reinforcement promotes a proactive, goal-oriented mentality that goes beyond pursuits of hobbies.

Hobbies have positive effects on one's physical health as well. A fun and interesting approach to keep active is to engage in activities like dance, hiking, or even gardening. Engaging in a pastime combined with regular physical exercise improves cardiovascular health, general well-being, and leads to a healthier lifestyle.

Hobbies are a perennial source of happiness for people of all ages. They provide a wide range of events and hobbies to pursue in retirement. Hobbies help students maintain a good work-life balance by offering a much-needed respite from the demands of the classroom. Professionals report lower stress levels and more job satisfaction when they participate in extracurricular activities.

Hobbies are very flexible; they may be tailored to fit certain interests and situations. There is a wide range of hobbies to fit a variety of interests, from quiet solo activities to exciting group events. The ability to customise hobbies to fit one's personality, interests, and resources is what makes them so beautiful.

In summary, engaging in hobbies is a dynamic and all-encompassing effort that extends beyond simple relaxation. It promotes individual development, creativity, and a feeling of belonging by encompassing cerebral, emotional, social, and physical aspects. Developing hobbies as a vital component of life is not only a luxury but also a necessary step towards building a balanced and contented life.

Stay Strong Mentally

Maintaining mental strength is a resilient and transforming path that entails developing coping strategies, cultivating a good outlook in the face of adversity, and tending to one's mental health. It's a comprehensive strategy that includes developing routines and practices that support mental toughness in addition to self-awareness and emotional intelligence.

The foundation of mental toughness is self-awareness. Comprehending their feelings, ideas, and responses enables people to face obstacles more clearly. This process of introspection include identifying thought patterns, accepting one's strengths and shortcomings, and adopting a realistic self-image. Self-awareness gives people the perspective they need to make wise choices and deal with challenges in a healthy way.

A key component of mental resilience is the development of emotional intelligence. This entails being sensitive to the feelings of others as well as identifying, comprehending, and controlling one's own emotions. People with emotional intelligence can skillfully manage interpersonal interactions, communicate, and resolve issues with poise and sensitivity. It offers a strong basis for preserving emotional balance in a variety of social situations.

Strong mental habits and routines are a major component of mental toughness. The foundations of physical well-being include regular exercise, enough sleep, and a balanced diet; these factors also have an effect on mental health. Stable foundations for emotional resilience are built via joyful activities, mindfulness or meditation practices, and regular daily routines. These practices support mental health and foster a good attitude on life.

Maintaining a robust mental health requires cultivating a growth attitude. Fostering a resilient attitude involves accepting obstacles, seeing setbacks as teaching moments, and continuing to believe in oneself. With this strategy, people may remain resilient in the face of adversity, adjust to change, and maintain their drive as they work towards their personal and professional objectives.

Mental toughness is greatly influenced by social ties. Having a network of friends, relatives, or mentors to lean on is a great help when things go hard. Feelings of loneliness are lessened when people communicate openly, ask for help, and express their emotions. Talking about experiences with others builds a community that supports personal resiliency.

The ability to manage stress is crucial for preserving mental toughness. This include learning useful coping techniques like deep breathing, meditation, or taking up a hobby. A balanced and reasonable workload is facilitated by prioritizing activities, setting realistic objectives, and developing the ability to say no when needed. Stress management strategies enable people to handle the pressures of life with calm and serenity.

Having an upbeat and cheerful outlook on life is a strong mental strength. A positive mindset is influenced by reframing negative ideas, practicing thankfulness, and concentrating on solutions rather than problems. Resilience is the ability to see setbacks as transient and solvable problems rather than as insurmountable roadblocks.

Maintaining mental health is a dynamic and deliberate process that calls for emotional intelligence, good habits, social connections, stress management, growth mindset, and an optimistic view in addition to self-awareness. It's a lifetime process of self-awareness and growth that equips people with the resilience, grace, and mental toughness needed to deal with life's challenges.

Mental Health Tips

It is essential to your general well-being to take care of your mental health. The following advice may assist in preserving mental wellness:

Make self-care a priority. Set aside time on a regular basis for enjoyable and calming self-care activities, like as reading, going for a stroll, or having a warm bath.

Create healthy routines: Keep up a regular daily schedule that includes exercise, balanced meals, and sleep schedules. A consistent schedule helps foster a feeling of control and regularity.

Remain Informed: Develop close social ties with your family and friends. Engage in meaningful interactions on a regular basis, and don't be afraid to ask for help when you need it.

Conscious Activities: Make meditation and mindfulness a part of your daily practice. You may handle stress, remain in the now, and have more mental clarity overall by using these techniques.

Reduce stressors: Determine the causes of stress in your life and take steps to reduce or manage them. This might include establishing limits, developing the ability to refuse requests, or, if needed, obtaining expert assistance.

Gratitude Verses: Practice self-affirmations to develop an optimistic outlook. Refute negative ideas and concentrate on your accomplishments and strong points.

Physical Activity: Studies have shown that regular exercise improves mental health. Make time for the things you like doing, like yoga, walking, or sports, and incorporate them into your daily schedule.

Nutritious Diet: Consume a diet rich in diverse nutrients and well-balanced. Certain diets, such as those high in omega-3 fatty acids, have been shown to improve mood and cognitive performance.

Ask for Expert Assistance: If you're suffering, don't hesitate to seek professional assistance. Mental health specialists such as therapists and counselors may provide invaluable support and resources.

Learn to Manage Your Time: To lessen emotions of overload, learn to manage your time effectively. Divide the work into more manageable chunks and rank the jobs according to significance.

Establish reasonable objectives: Set attainable short- and long-term objectives for yourself. To improve your sense of self-worth, acknowledge and appreciate your tiny victories.

Restrict Use of Technology: Set limits on technology usage to avoid becoming too dependent on screens and consuming too much information. Periodically cutting off may help maintain a more positive mental state.

Recall that each person's road towards mental wellness is unique. It's important to experiment and determine what suits you the best, and don't be afraid to ask for help when you need it.

Social Connections

Our lives are greatly impacted by our social ties, which affect both our general health and emotional well-being. Here is a thorough examination of the value of social ties as well as advice on how to create relationships that last:

Human Need at Birth: Humans have a basic desire for social connection that is present from birth. It has a profound impact on every aspect of human biology and psyche, from brain development to the control of emotions.

Social Assistance: One important source of emotional support is one's social network. Resiliently navigating life's problems may be facilitated by having friends and family who understand and support our sentiments.

De-stressing: Positive social connections have been shown to lower stress levels.

Oxytocin, a hormone that fosters bonding and lowers stress, is released in response to conversations, laughing, and shared experiences.

Benefits for Physical Health: Strong social relationships are related with improved physical health. According to research, those who have strong social networks often live longer, recover from illnesses more quickly, and have fewer chronic ailments.

Impact on Mental Health: Mental health is greatly impacted by social ties. Anxiety and sadness are among the mental health conditions that are associated with loneliness and social isolation. Conversely, consistent social connections support emotional health.

Enhanced Cognitive Function: Participating in social activities enhances cognitive performance. Our brains are challenged by meaningful interactions and social interactions, which encourage neuroplasticity and may lower the risk of cognitive decline.

Developing Compassion: Having conversations with a wide range of individuals fosters empathy. Comprehending other viewpoints cultivates a more empathetic and receptive outlook on the world.

A feeling of inclusion: Having social relationships gives one a feeling of community and belonging. Our sense of belonging to others builds a network of support that helps us to maintain our sense of self and mission.

Skills in Communication: Communication skills are improved via frequent social encounters. Whether we communicate verbally or nonverbally, social situation navigation improves our capacity for self-expression and mutual understanding.

Resolving Conflicts: Good social relationships provide important conflict-resolution abilities. Relationships are strengthened and personal development is promoted by learning how to resolve conflicts and misunderstandings.

Precision Above Quantity: The quality of the connections is just as important as their quantity. Time, effort, and a sincere connection are necessary for meaningful partnerships. Make an investment in connections that uplift and support you in life.

Acclimating to Shift: Our social network serves as a support system for adjusting to life's adjustments. A supporting social network makes transitions easier, whether one is relocating to a new area, changing occupations, or going through a crisis.

To sum up, fostering social ties is an intricate investment in our overall well being.

Make meaningful connections a priority, build a network of allies, and acknowledge the enormous influence that well-formed social networks can have on your life.

Learning and Growth

A constant process of gaining experiences, information, and abilities that support both career and personal progress, learning and growth are fundamental components of human development. Learning is an active process that takes place outside of the classroom and involves introspection, experimenting, and self-directed study.

When it comes to personal development, learning is a growth-promoting factor since it broadens one's perspective on the world and oneself. It encourages resilience and adaptation, enabling people to face obstacles in life from a wider angle. Accepting novel concepts and viewpoints fosters intellectual curiosity, which results in a deeper, more fulfilling life.

In today's environment of fast change, a dedication to lifelong learning is essential for success in the workplace. The dynamic nature of industry necessitates constant upskilling and adaptability. People who place a high value on lifelong learning are more likely to succeed in their jobs, remain current in their industries, and take advantage of new possibilities.

The digital era has completely changed education by providing never-before-seen access to tools and knowledge. People may customize their educational experiences to fit their own needs and interests by using online courses, webinars, and educational platforms. With the democratization of information, learning is now available to everybody with an internet connection and is no longer restricted to conventional classroom settings.

Furthermore, the growth mindset—a term made famous by psychologist Carol Dweck—emphasizes the conviction that aptitude and intellect can be enhanced by commitment and diligence. People that adopt this mentality see problems as chances to grow and learn rather than as insurmountable roadblocks, which fosters a positive feedback loop between learning and development.

Fostering a culture of learning in businesses increases worker creativity and engagement. Employers that place a high priority on employee development cultivate a staff that is capable of taking on new challenges in addition to being skilled at their existing duties. Ongoing education promotes a feeling of empowerment and accountability, which helps create an organizational structure that is more adaptable and durable.

In conclusion, learning and development are essential components of the human experience and are necessary for both career and personal progress. Adopting a perspective that prioritizes continuous education not only helps people deal with life's challenges but also cultivates an innovative and adaptable culture within companies and society at large.

Power of attorney

With the use of a power of attorney (POA), a person, sometimes referred to as the "agent" or "attorney-in-fact," may decide and act on behalf of another person, known as the "principal." This permission may be used for a wide range of tasks, such as dealing with financial, legal, and medical issues.

A versatile instrument, the power of attorney enables people to prepare for unanticipated events or to carry out particular transactions in the event that they are unable to act on their own. There are several kinds of power of attorney, and each has a special function.

With the extensive authority granted by a general power of attorney, the agent may manage a variety of matters on behalf of the principal. A restricted or specific power of attorney, on the other hand, limits the agent's ability to specified activities or during a predetermined window of time.

A durability provision in a power of attorney is an important component. In the event that the principle becomes incapable of making decisions, a durable power of attorney guarantees decision-making continuity. In the absence of this clause, the principal's authority may be terminated in the event that they lose mental ability.

Medical choices are explicitly covered by the healthcare power of attorney, sometimes known as the medical power of attorney. In situations when the principle is unable to express their desires, it gives the agent the power to make healthcare decisions. This document, which expresses choices for medical care and end-of-life care, is often included in advance care planning.

Because a power of attorney entails a great deal of trust, it should be created carefully. Since the agent will have the power to represent the principle in important situations, the principal should feel completely comfortable working with them. To make sure the document fits the principal's requirements and is compliant with local regulations, legal counsel is often advised.

In summary, a power of attorney is an effective legal tool that enables people to deal with a variety of life circumstances and prepare for the unexpected. Its adaptability and flexibility make it a useful tool for financial and personal planning, giving people an organized method to choose reliable people to represent them in court.

Stay Strong Physically

Keeping one's physical strength up is crucial for general health and has advantages that go far beyond building muscle. Strong physical health is linked to better mental and physical health as well as longer life spans. A comprehensive strategy that includes physical activity, healthy eating, rest, and thoughtful lifestyle decisions is needed to develop and maintain physical strength.

Engaging in regular physical exercise is essential for maintaining strength. A holistic approach to physical health is ensured by participating in a well-rounded fitness regimen that includes aerobic workouts, weight training, flexibility exercises, and balancing activities. This multimodal approach improves cardiovascular health, joint mobility, and general functional capability in addition to strengthening muscle.

Building and maintaining muscular mass is greatly aided by strength training in particular. It helps control weight by increasing strength and metabolism at the same time. Resistance training stimulates muscular fibres, fostering development and endurance, whether it is done with weights, resistance bands, or bodyweight. By increasing bone density, regular strength training may help reduce the risk of osteoporosis.

A healthy diet is essential for maintaining physical strength. A diet that is well-balanced and abundant in protein, carbs, healthy fats, vitamins, and minerals supplies the necessary ingredients for energy generation, muscle repair, and general health. Water promotes several physiological processes, facilitates healing, and helps sustain peak performance during physical activity, making it equally important to be hydrated.

Sufficient rest and recuperation are sometimes overlooked components of maintaining strength. After an exercise, muscles need time to rebuild and become stronger. This process depends critically on getting a good night's sleep since deep sleep is when growth hormone production peaks, which promotes muscle repair. Moreover, rest days in between strenuous sessions avoid overtraining and lower the chance of damage.

A mindful lifestyle, which includes stress reduction and abstaining from bad habits, greatly enhances physical strength. Prolonged stress may cause weariness, tense muscles, and slowed healing. Including methods of relaxation, such yoga or meditation, might lessen these impacts and enhance general wellbeing.

Physical health is also supported by abstaining from dangerous drugs like smoke and excessive alcohol use. For example, smoking impairs the transport of oxygen to muscles, which hinders their ability to operate and recover. Alcohol consumption should be restricted since too much of it might impair overall performance and the production of muscle protein.

In summary, maintaining physical strength requires a thorough and well-rounded strategy that includes consistent exercise, a healthy diet, enough sleep, and conscientious lifestyle decisions. People who embrace a holistic approach to physical well-being are able to develop and sustain their strength as well as reap the many interrelated advantages that go hand in hand with leading happy and healthy lives.

Managing stress and Anxiety

Maintaining mental health and general well-being requires effective stress and anxiety management. People may use a variety of methods and approaches to reduce stress and anxiety in their life.

1. Mindfulness and Meditation: Including meditation and mindfulness exercises in regular routines may be quite beneficial. By encouraging present-moment awareness, these approaches lessen the negative effects of anxious or stressful thoughts.

2. Deep Breathing Exercises: Deep breathing exercises assist in triggering the relaxation response in the body. Regular use of techniques like diaphragmatic breathing or box breathing may help lower anxiety levels.

3. Consistent Physical Activity: Being physically active is a great way to decompress. Endorphins are released during exercise and are naturally elevating hormones. Whether you choose to jog, stroll, or practice yoga on a daily basis, exercise may greatly help reduce stress.

4. A well-balanced diet A healthy, well-balanced diet is essential for mental wellness. There is evidence that eating certain foods, such those high in antioxidants and omega-3 fatty acids, might help reduce stress. Reducing sugar and caffeine consumption may also aid in mood stabilization.

5. Getting Enough Sleep: Getting enough sleep is crucial for mental health. Developing a regular sleep schedule and making sure you get enough sleep might help you handle stress more effectively. Stress and anxiety might worsen when there is little sleep.

6. Time Management: Overwhelming emotions may be avoided by establishing reasonable objectives and using time management techniques. One way to reduce the intimidating nature of jobs is to prioritize them and divide them into smaller, more achievable phases.

7. Social Assistance: Keeping up solid social ties is essential for stress and anxiety management. One way to release emotions and get insightful viewpoints is to speak with loved ones, friends, or a therapist.

8. Positive Self-Talk: One effective way to lower anxiety is to practice positive self-talk and confront negative ideas. Rephrasing unfavorable circumstances and affirmations might assist in changing one's viewpoint.

9. Hobbies and Calm hobbies: Reading, gardening, or listening to music are examples of enjoyable and peaceful hobbies that may serve as a healthy diversion and promote equilibrium.

10. Expert Assistance: It is proactive to seek support from mental health specialists, such as counselors or therapists. They may provide direction, coping mechanisms, and assistance based on the requirements of the person.

It's critical to understand that stress and anxiety management is a dynamic process, and that what works for one individual may not work for another. A more robust and stress-resistant lifestyle may be achieved by experimenting with different tactics and combining them into a holistic strategy. Regular self-care and mindfulness training are essential for promoting mental health.

Exercise and Fitness

A healthy lifestyle must include exercise and fitness since they have several psychological, emotional, and physical advantages. Exercise has several benefits beyond only burning calories; it may also enhance cardiovascular health, physical strength, flexibility, and mental wellness.

Running, swimming, and cycling are examples of cardiovascular exercises that raise the heart rate and improve the cardiovascular system's efficiency. Frequent aerobic exercise reduces the risk of cardiovascular illnesses by strengthening the heart, lowering blood pressure, and improving circulation. Moreover, aerobic workouts trigger the body's natural mood enhancers, endorphins, which enhance wellbeing and lower stress.

Strength training promotes physical strength and endurance by focusing on certain muscle groups via resistance exercises like weightlifting, bodyweight exercises, or resistance band routines. Increasing lean muscle mass speeds up metabolism, which helps with weight control in addition to giving you a more toned body. Strength training also improves functional ability in everyday tasks, lowers the chance of injury, and promotes bone health.

Yoga and other flexibility exercises help to increase muscle suppleness and joint range of motion. Improved flexibility helps with posture, eases muscular stress, and lowers the risk of injury. Stretching exercises improve general mobility and agility, which are essential for leading an independent and active life. They should be included into any training programme.

Exercises for stability and balance are essential, particularly as people age. Exercises designed to improve proprioception, preserve equilibrium, and avoid falls include tai chi. By improving functional fitness, these workouts help people do everyday chores confidently and easily.

Exercise has significant advantages for mental health. Dopamine and serotonin are two neurotransmitters that are released when you exercise and are linked to happier moods and less depressive and anxious symptoms. Frequent exercise has also been connected to improvements in memory, focus, and brain function in general.

People may customize their fitness regimens to match their objectives and personal tastes because of the variety of workout alternatives available. The secret is to choose pleasurable and long-lasting activities, whether you want to participate in team sports, group fitness programmes, outdoor activities, or solitary exercises. This guarantees sustained compliance with an exercise programme and infuses enjoyment into the process of achieving better health.

Furthermore, wearable technology that tracks and motivates users, fitness applications, and virtual exercises have completely changed the fitness environment. With the help of these tools—which provide social connectedness, customized training regimens, and real-time feedback—exercise becomes more enjoyable and accessible to a wider variety of people.

To sum up, fitness and exercise are the cornerstones of a happy and healthy existence. Embracing a well-rounded strategy that combines aerobic, strength, flexibility, and balance exercises not only improves physical well-being but also adds to mental resilience and general quality of life. People may take a revolutionary step towards a better and happier life by including regular physical exercise into their everyday routines.

Healthy Lifestyle Choices

A comprehensive commitment to making decisions that enhance one's physical, mental, and emotional well-being is necessary to adopt a healthy lifestyle. These decisions include a wide range of topics, including social interactions, stress reduction, sleep, and physical activity in addition to diet and exercise.

The foundation of a healthy lifestyle is nutrition. For the body to operate at its best, a balanced, diverse diet full of fruits, vegetables, whole grains, lean proteins, and healthy fats is necessary. Reducing the risk of chronic illnesses and managing weight may be achieved via reducing excessive consumption of processed foods, carbohydrates, and saturated fats and by making educated decisions regarding portion sizes.

Another essential component is regular physical exercise. Combining aerobic workouts with strength training, flexibility exercises, and mindful movement benefits mental wellness in addition to physical fitness. Exercise causes endorphins to be released, which improves mood, lowers stress levels, and improves cognitive performance in general.

Getting enough sleep is a critical but often overlooked component of leading a healthy lifestyle. Recuperation from physical injuries, memory consolidation, and emotional control all depend on getting enough sleep. Having regular sleep schedules and a sleep-friendly atmosphere are important for general health and energy.

Managing stress effectively is essential in the fast-paced world of today. Methods like yoga, deep breathing, meditation, and taking up a hobby may all help reduce stress and encourage relaxation. A robust response to life's problems includes establishing a positive outlook, setting realistic objectives, and striking a balance between work and play.

An encouraging social network and strong social ties are important for mental and emotional well-being. Developing and preserving connections with friends, family, and the community helps people feel less alone, gives them a sense of community, and is an essential support system in trying times.

It's essential to give up bad habits like smoking and binge drinking if you want to lead a healthy lifestyle. These behaviors impair mental and physical health in addition to raising the risk of chronic illnesses. Adopting a moderate and tobacco-free drinking strategy promotes lifespan and general health.

Preventive care and routine health examinations are crucial for the early identification and treatment of any health problems. Proactive health management includes keeping track of blood pressure and cholesterol levels as well as having up to date immunization records.

Navigating life's uncertainties requires resilience and a positive mentality. Emotional well-being is influenced by cultivating a sense of purpose, being grateful, and seeing obstacles as chances for personal development. Maintaining a good balance in life also requires prioritising self-care and establishing limits.

To sum up, leading a healthy lifestyle involves making decisions that support one's physical, mental, and emotional well. People may start a life-changing path towards a healthier and more happy existence by including preventative healthcare, good social relationships, regular exercise, enough sleep, balanced eating, and efficient stress management into their daily routines.

Regular Health Checkups

Proactive healthcare relies heavily on routine health examinations, which have several advantages beyond early illness identification. These checks, also known as preventive or regular screenings, play a key role in the early diagnosis, treatment, and prevention of possible health disorders, adding to overall well-being.

Above all, routine health examinations help in the early identification of medical disorders. In their early stages, many illnesses, such as some malignancies, cardiovascular problems, and metabolic abnormalities, may not show any symptoms at all. Regular examinations, such blood tests, mammograms, colonoscopies, and cholesterol assessments, allow medical practitioners to spot anomalies or risk factors before they become more significant health issues.

Regular checkups that promote preventive healthcare provide people the ability to take charge of their health. People may reduce possible health risks by adopting educated lifestyle choices by recognising risk factors or early indicators of illnesses. This might include following any prescribed medical treatments or drugs as well as making changes to one's diet, exercise routine, and stress management style.

The treatment of chronic illnesses is aided by routine health examinations. Routine monitoring enables medical professionals to evaluate the efficacy of treatment regimens for patients with pre-existing conditions, make required modifications, and provide prompt interventions. For those managing chronic conditions, this proactive approach improves overall quality of life and helps avoid problems.

Additionally, regular examinations and screenings can avoid illnesses by modifying lifestyle choices and obtaining vaccines. Vaccinations lower the risk of sickness and possible epidemics by providing protection against a number of infectious illnesses. To lower the risk of chronic illnesses, healthcare providers may also offer advice on preventative measures including stress management, regular exercise, and keeping a healthy weight.

Healthcare professionals have the chance to give individualized health advice and counseling throughout these examinations. Talks on diet, physical activity, mental health, and other lifestyle aspects that affect general wellbeing are included in this. In order to enhance their health results, patients may get advice on forming better behaviors and implementing long-lasting changes.

Frequent check-ups are another way to help manage healthcare resources in an economical and effective manner. The need for more involved and costly therapies may be decreased by early identification and intervention, which can stop illnesses from progressing to more severe stages. This enhances the effectiveness of the healthcare system as a whole in addition to helping individuals.

Additionally, health examinations are essential for fostering a culture of preventative healthcare. Promoting regular screenings as a top priority helps people adopt a proactive attitude towards their health. A population that is more conscious of their health and actively involved in preserving and enhancing their well-being is a result of this cultural transformation.

To sum up, regular physical examinations are an essential part of proactive medical treatment. Routine screenings allow people to take charge of their health, make educated lifestyle decisions, and contribute to the overall efficacy and efficiency of the healthcare system by enabling the early identification, prevention, and treatment of health issues. Making routine health examinations a priority is an investment in one's health that will pay off in terms of long-term vigor and health..

Retirement age

Over time, as society expectations, economic conditions, and demography have changed, so too has the idea of retirement age. Retirement age is the average age at which people stop working full-time, signalling the end of their working years and the beginning of a period of life that is often marked by leisure, personal interests, and, most of the time, financial independence.

Retirement age was traditionally established at a fixed age, usually around 65, and was greatly affected by the creation of social security and pension programmes. But the idea of a set retirement age has grown less strict and more individualised in today's culture. This change is the result of several causes, such as longer life expectancies, advancements in healthcare, and people's desire to continue being actively involved in their older years.

The rising flexibility of retirement age is one notable trend. In an effort to enjoy their latter years while in good health and following particular hobbies, some people decide to retire early. However, others choose to retire later because of monetary concerns, a strong sense of purpose in their job, or a want to carry on making a positive impact on their communities and professions.

The decision of when to retire is heavily influenced by financial factors. The sufficiency of retirement funds, investment portfolios, and pension plans frequently impacts the choice regarding when to retire. People need to properly prepare for retirement because of the complexity of today's financial environments. This will help them make sure they have enough money for their preferred lifestyle and any future medical requirements.

Retirement age is also influenced by social security programmes and government regulations. Retirement age and eligibility for state pensions or other social benefits are related in various nations. When people decide to retire may be greatly impacted by changes to these laws, such as increasing the official retirement age to accommodate demographic swings and financial issues.

Phased retirement is a popular idea that lets people go to part-time work or progressively cut down on hours worked before retiring completely. This strategy makes it easier for people to move into retirement while preserving their sense of purpose, social networks, and financial security.

Retirement's psychological and emotional effects must be taken into account. Some people look forward to retirement as a time for leisure, travel, and catching up on long-abandoned hobbies. Others, on the other hand, could worry about identity, purpose, and the possibility of social isolation while considering retirement. Making arrangements for these non-monetary factors is crucial to guaranteeing a happy retirement.

Retirement has also been impacted by the way that work is evolving, with a focus on flexible and remote work. Some people could decide to go on working in a reduced capacity while starting their own businesses, consulting, or freelancing. The concept of retiring age is being challenged by the "unretirement" movement, which offers new opportunities for sustained production and fulfilment.

Retirement age is a dynamic and unique part of modern life that is impacted by a variety of circumstances such as government legislation, health issues, financial concerns, and changing views on labor and leisure. A seamless and fulfilling move into this stage of life depends on thorough preparation that takes into account lifestyle, financial, and emotional factors when people decide when to retire.

Wills and trust

The two most important legal tools for estate planning are wills and trusts. A will specifies how a person's possessions should be allocated when they pass away. It usually identifies the beneficiaries, appoints an executor to carry out the intentions, and sometimes addresses guardianship of younger siblings.

Conversely, trusts are legal bodies that keep and administer resources on behalf of people or institutions. They may be alive or testamentary, revocable or irrevocable. Testamentary trusts are formed by a will and only come into force after the grantor's passing, while living trusts are created during the grantor's lifetime and are modifiable.

The ability of trusts to bypass probate, a drawn-out and expensive legal procedure, is one of its benefits. A will must be validated during probate in order for assets to be distributed under court supervision. If adequately financed, trusts circumvent this procedure, enabling a more rapid and confidential transfer of assets.

Trusts are flexible as well. Specialised trusts, such charity or spendthrift trusts, let grantors customize agreements to meet particular requirements. They also provide a seamless transfer of power in the event that the grantor becomes incapable of managing assets.

Another thing to think about is estate taxes. With a thoughtful asset transfer, trusts may reduce tax obligations. This is particularly important for wealthy people who have large estate taxes to pay.

Although they have different functions, trusts and wills may work well together in complete estate planning. A trust simplifies the transfer of most assets, but a will acts as a safety net for those assets not covered by the trust.

It's critical to regularly examine and update these records to account for life events like births, weddings, and substantial changes in finances. It is recommended to get advice from legal experts with expertise in estate planning to make sure that papers comply with current regulations and successfully accomplish their intended purposes.

In the end, building a thorough estate plan that suits a person's particular circumstances and goals requires considerable thought and expert advice due to the intricacy of wills and trusts.

Recommendations planing

Early and proactive preparation is essential when it comes to retirement planning. Start by evaluating your debts, assets, and savings as well as your existing financial status. Make a thorough budget to comprehend your spending and pinpoint places where you may increase your savings.

To reduce risk, diversify your investing portfolio. Depending on your time horizon and risk tolerance, take into account a combination of stocks, bonds, and other assets. Review and modify your investing portfolio on a regular basis.

Increase your contributions to retirement accounts that provide tax advantages, such IRAs and 401(k)s. Employer-sponsored plans may help you save more for retirement, so take advantage of them and any matching contributions they may provide.

Make sure you know exactly what you want out of retirement. Establish your retirement living goals and calculate the expenses involved. This will assist you in determining a reasonable savings goal.

Keep yourself updated on changes in the financial scene so you may modify your plan as needed. Pay attention to any changes in legislation, interest rates, and market developments that might affect your retirement funds.

Think about speaking with a financial expert to get tailored guidance based on your particular circumstances. They can guide you through difficult financial choices and make sure your retirement plan is in line with your goals.

Review your retirement plan on a regular basis to account for life events like marriage, having kids, or unforeseen bills. To remain on course, make any necessary adjustments to your savings and investing plan.

Finally, keep in mind the expense of healthcare during retirement. Examine your alternatives for healthcare coverage, including Medicare and supplementary insurance, and budget for probable medical costs.

Keep in mind that maintaining financial stability throughout your elderly years involves regular work and thoughtful revisions to a well-thought-out retirement plan.

Conclusion

InIn conclusion, taking a deliberate and planned strategy is necessary to start the retirement journey and stay strong throughout. Careful financial preparation to ensure a secure future, supporting personal development and discovery, putting health and well-being first, creating meaningful social ties, and adjusting to changing circumstances are the essential tasks. By taking these actions, people may ensure that their retirement years are a chapter of ongoing strength and satisfaction rather than merely a time of relaxation. They can also nurture resilience and vitality in addition to retiring comfortably.